decorating with
pattern

katrin cargill

photography by **james merrell**

decorating with
pattern

katrin cargill

photography by **james merrell**

RYLAND
PETERS
& SMALL

In memory of **Rufus**, who gave me eleven
years of unstinting love, humorous cheer
and boundless affection.

Art Director **Jacqui Small**

Art Editor **Penny Stock**

Project Designer **Lucy Hamilton**

Editor **Toria Leitch**

Production **Kate Mackillop**

Main Text by **Amicia de Moubray**

First Published in Great Britain in 1997
by Ryland Peters & Small
Cavendish House, 51–55 Mortimer Street, London
W1N 7TD

Text © Katrin Cargill 1997
Design and photographs © Ryland Peters & Small
1997

Produced by Mandarin Offset, Hong Kong
Printed in Hong Kong

ISBN 1 900518 28 7

A CIP record for this book is available from the
British Library

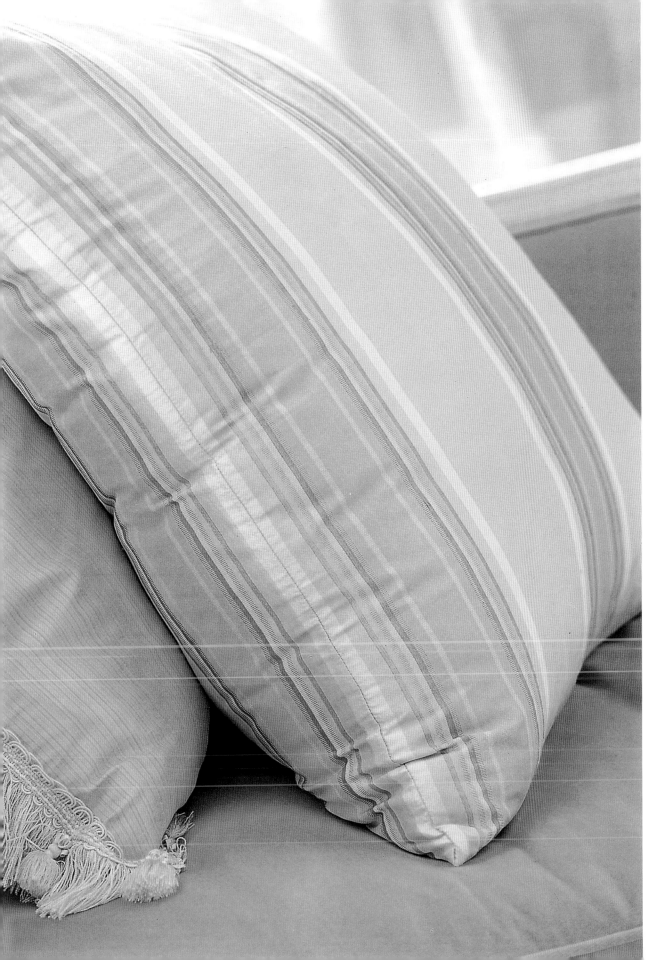

contents

PATTERN SURROUNDS OUR LIVES. SOME OF US ARE MORE AWARE OF IT THAN OTHERS. A LOT OF US ARE INTIMIDATED BY IT – DO I DARE USE THAT GORGEOUS

large-scaled damask on my sofa or shall I play it safe and use a neutral linen, or perhaps be a little brave and use a tiny dotted pattern? Then what do I use for the curtains, the chairs, what do I put on the walls? Bewildering thoughts to most people. Why is it that some combinations work and others don't? Why does a little check so successfully enhance a *toile de Jouy*, or a broad stripe work so well with a damask? It's something akin to the golden rule of proportions. Some patterns just work together and some are better isolated. Scale plays a crucial role in the successful use of pattern. Presented with a huge room a professional designer will tend to use an overscaled pattern or a strong colour; while a small room might be similarly treated with the use of a large pattern such as an overbroad stripe, it is probably wise used in neutral colours, or in two tones of one colour. This creates an illusion of scale and hence space.

This book sets out to illustrate lots of beautiful examples of mixes of fabrics and patterns to inspire you to use pattern more confidently. We show rooms where one pattern entirely creates the mood, such as a stylized floral stripe used on walls and windows alike, or where one colour is used in many textures: linen mixed with wool, suede with cotton, or quilted cotton with crewel work.

Here is a celebration of truly wonderful classic patterns that are dear to my heart and are shown in innumerable different settings in specially commissioned photographs taken on location in both America and Europe. There are no do's and don'ts here; decorating is all about having fun and creating an environment which is uplifting to be in. Even the most experienced of top international tastebrokers have been known to agonize about which fabrics to use and what goes with what. It can be an overawing experience. So the aim of this book is to offer a rich source of inspiration for

decorating ideas by illustrating and explaining many examples of all types of interiors where patterns have been happily mixed, sometimes with a little daring too.

Each chapter fully explores its pattern theme – from textures to stripes, to checks, to motifs and pictorials – taking into account its history, its practicality and how it can be used either on its own or combined with others in a diverse range of styles, from smart international chic to humble rural cottage interiors in America, Sweden, France, Italy and England. Confidence with pattern can be gained through experience but as very few people have the time these days to try out endless different combinations I have tried here to gather together a host of decorating ideas based around the five main categories of pattern found in the home.

A roomful of happily co-existing patterns: *toile de Jouy* is visible, alongside an African kente chosen for the tablecloth, and traditional striped upholstery on a chair.

Throughout the book I have interspersed ten exciting projects that are easy to do, with clear and simple step-by-step instructions so that you can instantly set about bringing pattern into your home.

The possibilities are endless. Good luck!

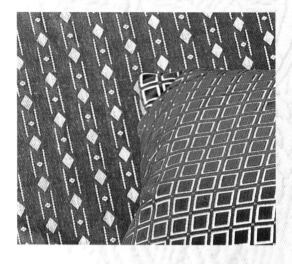  

We perceive texture
visually through the play of light
on a surface and physically
through touch. This is the
sensual dimension of decorating
where smooth silks, breezy
cottons and coarse matting
all have their place.

texture

Textiles made with self-woven designs are undoubtedly the most subtle way of introducing pattern into your home. With these fabrics the pattern is incorporated into the material either as it is woven, in the case of fabrics such as damask or waffle weave cotton, or else applied afterwards, as it is with devorée velvets where the pattern is burnt into the fabric.

The evolution of weaving techniques over the course of the centuries has resulted in a vast array of materials whose pattern and texture is solely dependent on the intricacies of the weave. As methods have become more sophisticated, so have some of the weaves. The spectrum ranges from fabrics, such as finely embossed muslins, whose pattern is barely discernible to the naked eye, to the truly opulent textures of richly-hued gaufrage velvets.

Left **A silk damask cushion cover has a thick fringe to complement the richness of the fabric and provides a striking contrast to the chair it sits on.** Above **The texture of the cream carpet is its most striking feature; the monochromatic repeat is an example of a subtle but effective use of pattern.**

Although we tend to be conservative in the way we combine textures in our homes, we find it easy to experiment with our clothing. We need no extra confidence when it comes to wearing a silk shirt with a pair of trousers made from herringbone tweed, completing the outfit with a devorée velvet scarf. So why should we find it so difficult to combine these same textures in our homes? Be inspired by the seemingly haphazard assortment of fabrics hanging in your wardrobe and apply the same principles to decorating. Remember that there is only one rule when it comes to decorating your own home and that is that the environment you create must be one in which you feel comfortable and which reflects your personality. If you want to create an arrangement using a delicate moiré silk in combination with a rough burlap in the same room, it is perfectly fine, as long as it looks and feels right to you.